Samsung Galaxy Z Flip 5 (5G) User Guide

The Comprehensive Step-by-Step and Illustrated Manual for Beginners and Seniors to Master the Samsung Galaxy Flip 5 Smartphone with Tips and Tricks

Shawn Blaine

Table of Contents

Introduction

On the foldable screen of the Galaxy Flip 5, there's a 6.7-inch OLED panel that features a refresh rate of 120 Hz and a resolution of 1080p.

The outer screen used to be called the Cover Display in previous iterations but has been renamed the "Flex Window." The company has restyled it and even made it larger at 3.4 inches. The Flex Window display resolution stands at 720p with a refresh rate of 60 Hz.

You can now do so much with it without having to unfold the device. There will be over thirteen widgets designed specifically for the Flex Window. So, you'll be able to carry out quick operations such as making payments with the Samsung Wallet without having to unfold the device. You'll also be able to capture selfies with the back cameras, reply to text messages, and so on, even with the smartphone folded.

The Flex Window also has a "Labs" section where, along with these thirteen widgets, you can also access some applications such as WhatsApp and Google Maps.

You'll also be able to open several applications directly from the Flex Window, but the functionality of the app on the small display will differ from app to app.

If desired, you can adjust the color palette of the Flex Window to be the same as that of the Galaxy

Flip colorway or to reflect your mood at a specific time.

The phone can be propped up in a semi-unfolded position, called Flex Mode, allowing hands-free capturing of photos.

Just like the Galaxy Flip 4, Samsung has added two cameras (12 megapixels wide and 12 megapixels ultrawide) to the rear of the smartphone.

The front-facing 10-megapixel camera, housed in a circular cutout at the upper section of the inner screen, uses the same sensors as its predecessor. Samsung has also improved the hinge; both sides of the smartphone can now fold completely flat without leaving any gaps.

The smartphone comes with the Snapdragon 8 Gen 2 processor and 8GB of RAM, while the battery capacity stands at 3,700 mAh, which is the same as its predecessor.

This book was written to help you operate your Galaxy Flip 5 like an expert. The information you need to know is clearly laid out. With this, you will be able to set up and navigate your Galaxy Flip seamlessly and optimally.

Chapter One

Set up Galaxy Z Flip

- Put a 5G SIM card into your Samsung Galaxy Flip.
- Follow up by pressing the power button to turn the smartphone on after inserting the SIM card.
- Once your Galaxy Flip powers on, choose your preferred language from the "Welcome" menu that appears.
- After that, press the "**Start**" button.

- Go through the instructions and check the needed options.

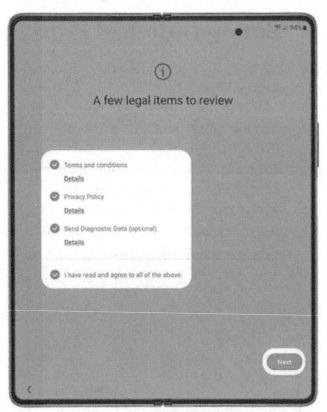

- Thereafter, press "**Next**."
- After that, touch "**Next**."

- If prompted, enter the PIN and continue with the on-screen instructions.
- Follow up by selecting a wireless network and entering its password.
- Press "**Skip**" to discard connection to any wireless network.
- On the next menu, press "**Next**."

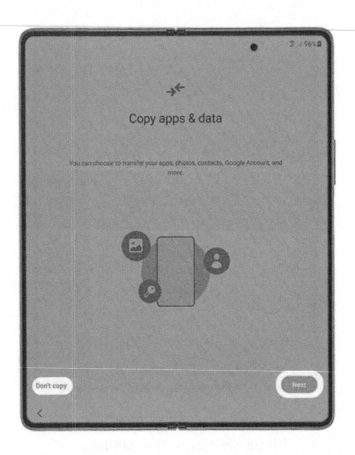

- Ensure your old device is with you, then press "**Next**."
- To discard copying files from the old device, press "**Don't copy**."
- Follow up by signing into your Google account. Go ahead and create one if you don't have an account already.
- If you desire to add an account later, choose "**Skip**."

- On the "Google Services" menu, turn on the required toggles, then press "**Accept**."

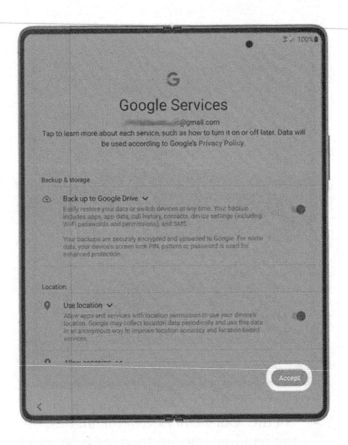

- From the "**Protect your phone**" interface, select any of the desired options that you wish to secure your device, then go through the prompts.
- Press "**Skip**" if you desire to add any of the listed security options at a later time.

- On the next menu, press "**I agree**" to set up Google Assistant. To do this at a later time, choose "**Skip**."

- While on the menu requiring access to the Assistant, press "**I agree**." Otherwise, press "**Skip**" to do it later.
- Follow up by turning on the required toggles to activate or deactivate the listed options.
- After that, press "**Accept**."
- Go through the onscreen prompts to set up the smartphone.
- After the setup is complete, choose "**Done**."

Power Off the Phone

- If you need to shut down your smartphone, long-tap the side and volume down buttons simultaneously for a few seconds.
- Once the power menu shows, press "**Power Off**" or "**Restart**."
- To power it back on, press the Side button.

Charge the Galaxy Flip

- Start by inserting one side of the charger into the smartphone, then insert the other part into a power outlet.

- If the battery icon shows, it means the smartphone is being charged.

Enable Wireless PowerShare

Wireless PowerShare is a feature that enables users of Samsung devices to charge their smartphones and accessories with another Galaxy smartphone.

- Head to the Settings app.

- In there, press "**Battery and device care**."

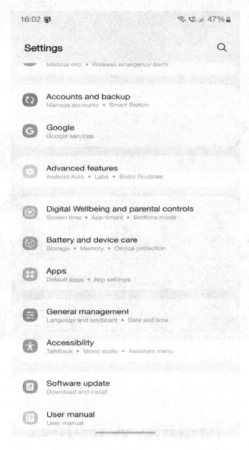

- Thereafter, press "**Battery**."

- Next up, press "**Wireless power sharing**."

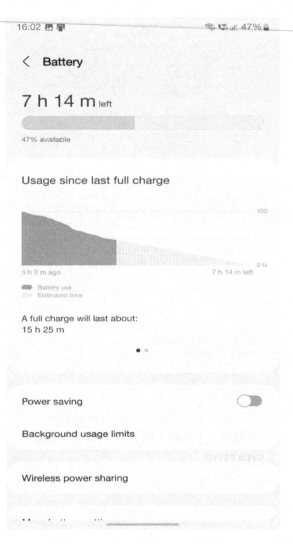

- Press the toggle next to "**Off**" to activate the Wireless power sharing.

< Wireless power sharing

Off

Put the centre of your phone back to back with another device.
If you have trouble connecting or charging is slow, remove any
cover from each device.

• Using this feature may affect call reception or data services,
  depending on your network environment.
• Works with most Qi-compatible devices. Different devices may
  charge at different speeds.

Battery limit
30%

Charging will stop when your phone reaches the battery
percentage you set.

- At this point, you should turn the Galaxy Flip so that the screen is facing down.
- Follow up by placing the Samsung accessory or phone in the middle of your Galaxy Flip.
- Arrange both devices such that their charging coils come into contact and transmit power wirelessly.
- Once both devices are properly aligned, charging will begin immediately.

17

Add Battery Limit

If you wish to enter the battery limit at which wireless charging will automatically stop, then add a battery limit.

- Head to the Settings app.
- In there, press "**Battery and device care**."
- After that, press "**Battery**."
- Thereafter, press "**Wireless power sharing**."
- From there, press "**Battery limit**."
- Follow up by selecting your desired limit.
- Next up, press "**OK**."

Chapter Two

Backup and Restore Files

Saving a copy of your Galaxy Flip files and content can come in handy when you misplace the phone or it gets damaged beyond repair. With a backup, you can still see your files on any device and restore them when needed.

Use Samsung Account for Backup

- Head to the Settings app.
- Next up, press "**Accounts and backup**."
- In there, touch "**Backup data**" below the "**Samsung Cloud**" heading.
- Follow up by choosing the app you desire to back up.
- Next up, press "**Back up now**."
- After that, press "**Done**."

Restore Files from your Samsung Account

- Head to the Settings app.
- Next up, press "**Accounts and backup**."
- Thereafter, press "**Restore data**."
- Proceed by selecting the backup you desire to restore.
- In there, press "**Restore**."

- Next up, press "**Install**" to retrieve your app screen.

Backup with a Google account
- Head to the Settings app.
- Thereafter, choose "**Accounts and backup**."
- After that, press "**Back up data**" below the "**Google Drive**" heading.
- Thereafter, press "**Back up now**."

Use Smart Switch to Send and Backup Files

With Smart Switch, you can easily export your photos, contacts, calendar, phone settings, and more to your new device. There's also support for backing up to a local computer or an external drive.

Send Files Wirelessly from an old Device

While using Smart Switch to export or import data, ensure your devices are plugged into a power outlet to charge.

Also, ensure that the Smart Switch application is running on both devices and that both devices are nearby.

- Head to the Settings app.
- Next up, press "**Accounts and backup**."

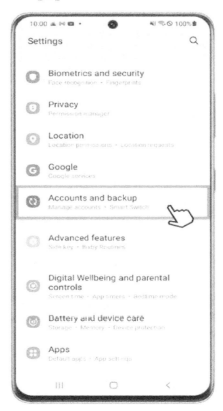

- From there, press "**Bring data from old device**."

- From your newest phone, press "**Receive data**."

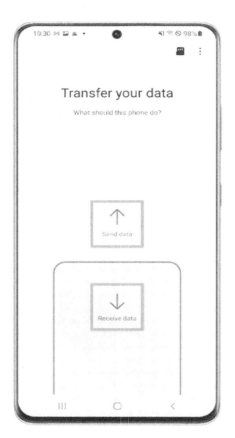

- From your older phone, press "**Send data**."
- Choose the type of smartphone you're using.

- After that, press "**Wireless**."

- On the older phone, head to the Smart Switch application to pair. Press "**Allow**" to approve the connection.
- Follow up by pressing the files to transfer.
- After that, press "**Transfer**."
- Once the transfer is done, press "**Go to the Home screen**."

Transfer Files from an iPhone via iCloud

- Launch the Smart Switch application on the newest phone.
- In there, choose "**Receive data**."
- After this, choose "**iPhone/iPad**."
- Next up, press "**Get data from iCloud instead**."
- Follow up by filling in your iCloud ID and password.
- Thereafter, press "**Sign in**."
- Proceed by inserting the verification code.
- After that, choose "**OK**."
- Go ahead and select the data you desire to transfer.
- Then, press "**Import**."
- Hit on "**Import**" again.

Transfer Files via a USB Cable

- Start by connecting your newest phone and the older phone with a USB cable.
- From the displayed menu, press "**Smart Switch**."
- After that, press "**Receive data**."
- From your oldest phone, press "**Allow**."
- At this point, the newest phone will detect the old one.
- The list of items you can export will be displayed, choose them and press "**Transfer**."

- After the transfer is complete, remove the connected cable.

Chapter Three

Restore the Phone to Factory Settings

Whenever you perform a factory data reset, your smartphone will delete all of its data and go back to its original settings. Only do this once you have backed up your files.

- Head to the Settings app.
- Right there, press "**General management**."

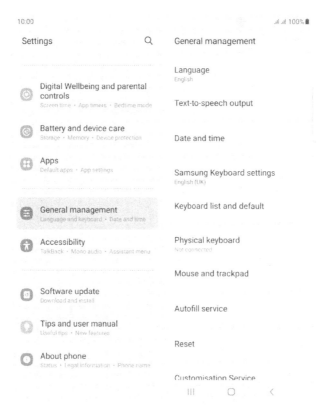

- Now, press "**Reset**."

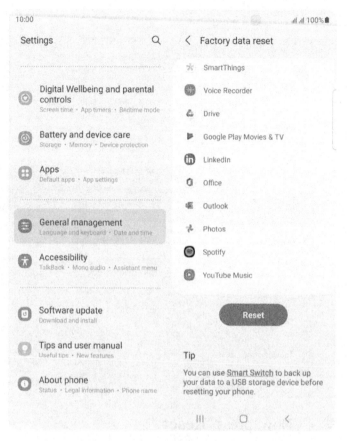

- Thereafter, press **"Factory data reset."**
- Next up, press **"Reset."**
- From there, press **"Delete all."**

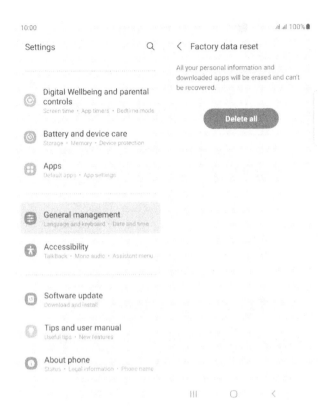

Reset your Network Settings

It is best to reset your network settings if you're having connection problems. This will reset your mobile data, Wi-Fi networks, and other preferences.

- Head to the Settings app.
- In there, press "**General management**."
- After that, press "**Reset**."
- Next up, press "**Reset network settings**."
- Thereafter, press "**Reset settings**."
- After which, press "**Reset**."

Activate Secure Wi-Fi

To safeguard your Wi-Fi connection and avoid hackers preying on it when using a public Wi-Fi network, you can enable the Secure Wi-Fi feature.

- Head to the Settings app.
- Thereafter, touch "**Biometrics and security**."
- After this, touch "**Secure Wi-Fi**."
- Then, choose "**Continue**."
- Go through the guide, then authorize access.
- Tap "Protect" the moment you start browsing.
- If you need to see your existing plan, touch "**Protection plan**."

- Hit on "**Upgrade**" if you need to sign up for a new plan. With the free plan, you only get Secure Wi-Fi for 1024MB/month.
- While on the Secure Wi-Fi menu, select "**Auto protect Wi-Fi**" to automatically encrypt your browsing while using public networks. Press the switch to enable it.
- You can choose to add Secure Wi-Fi to selected apps only. If so, press the three dots. After that, choose "**Settings**." Next up, select "**Protected apps**." Press the switch beside an app to enable the **Secure Wi-Fi** protection.
- If you need to view your usage, tap "**Protection activity**.

Activate Screen Time Out

To set when your screen will go blank after inactivity, you should select a duration for the screen timeout.

- Head to the Settings app.
- Then, press "**Display**."

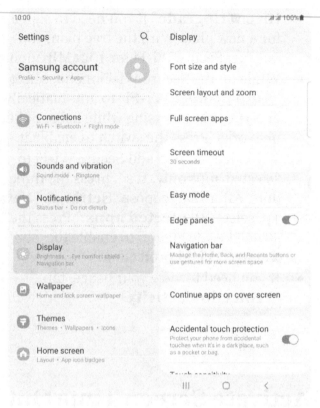

- After that, press "**Screen timeout**."
- Follow up by choosing your desired duration.

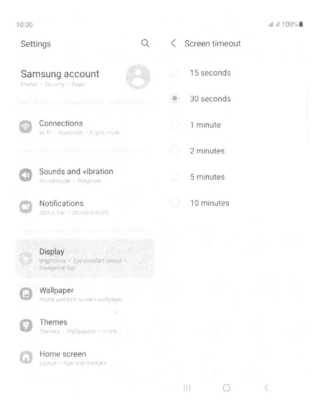

Enable Ring Tone

- Head to the Settings app.
- After that, press "**Sounds and vibration**."

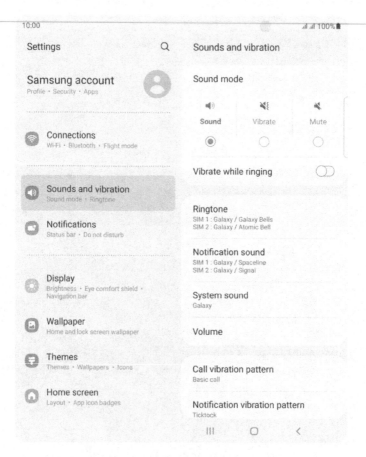

- In there, touch "**Ringtone**."
- Press the appropriate SIM.

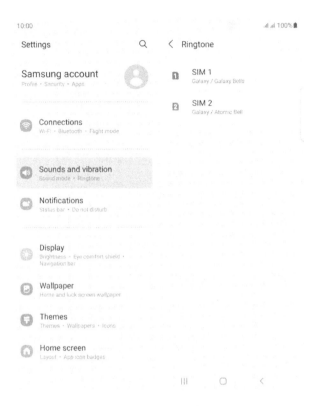

- Then, choose from the listed ringtone.
- To import, press the plus icon.

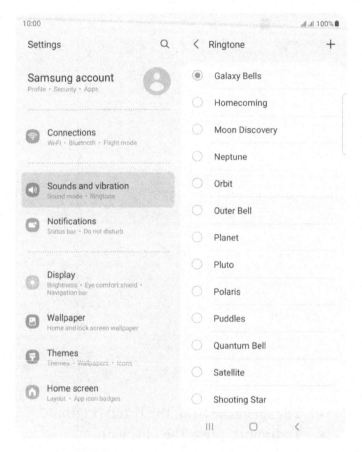

- Go ahead and choose a ringtone.
- Then, press **"Done."**

Change the Font

Right in the Settings app, you can adjust the text size and style of your smartphone.

- Head to the Settings app.

- Thereafter, touch "**Font size and style**."
- Next up, press "**Font size and style**" again.
- Touch the required setting to choose an option.
- Move the slider sideways to change the text size.
- Press the switch beside "**Bold font**" to activate or deactivate it.
- To change the text style, press "**Font style**."

Add Language

- Head to the Settings app.
- Right there, press "**General management**."

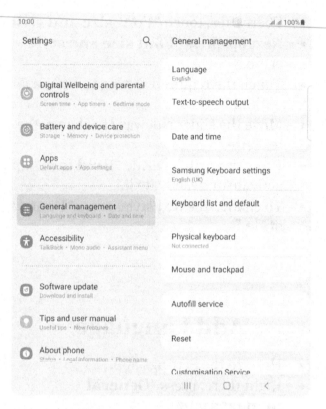

- Thereafter, press "**Language**."
- Next up, press "**Add language**."

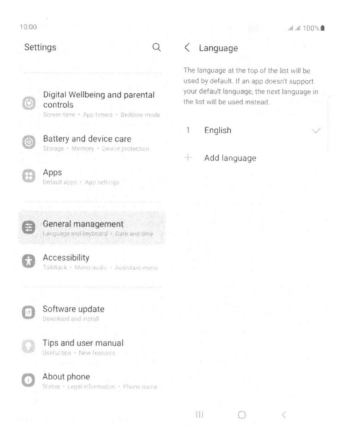

- Choose from the listed languages.

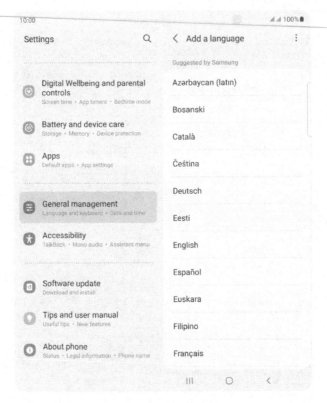

- To make the selected language the default for your smartphone, press "**Set as default**."
- Thereafter, press "**Apply**."

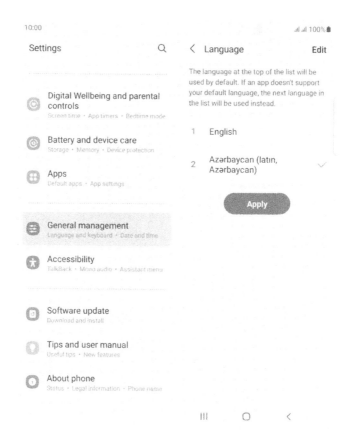

Turn on Notifications

To make your smartphone buzz whenever you get a notification, you should activate notifications.

- Head to the Settings app.
- In there, press "**Notifications**."

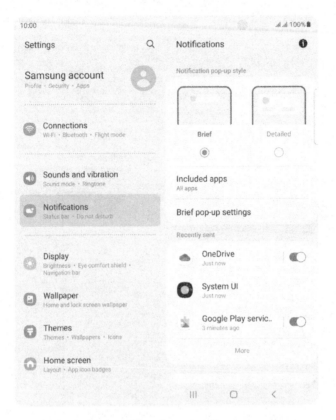

- After that, press "**More**."
- From the listed apps, press the toggle beside them to turn on alerts for the desired apps.

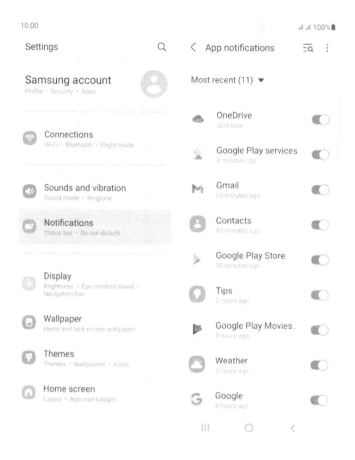

Add Lock Code

By setting up a lock code on your smartphone, only you can unlock it and access its content.

- Head to the Settings app.
- Then, press "**Lock screen**."

45

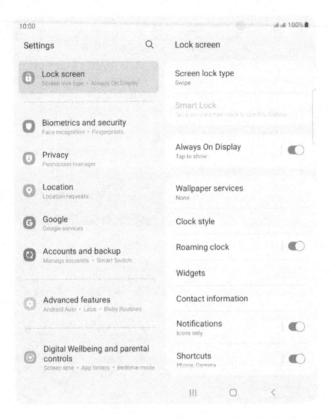

- Right there, press **"Screen lock type."**

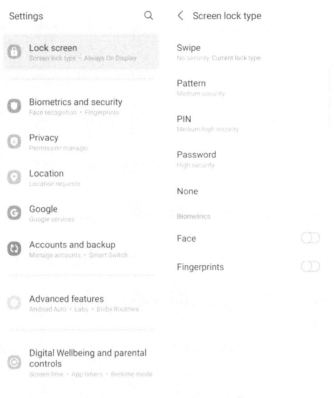

- Next up, press "**Fingerprints**."
- Thereafter, touch "**Continue**."

Fingerprints

A quick and easy way to unlock your phone and verify yourself in apps.
Your fingerprint data is secured by Knox.

- Follow up by pressing your desired lock code.
- Go through the onscreen guide to add another lock code.

<   Set secure screen lock

Before you can register your fingerprints, you need to set a secure screen lock (pattern, PIN, or password).

Remember it. You'll need it to unlock your phone after it restarts and occasionally at other times to ensure your phone is secure.

Pattern
Medium security

PIN
Medium-high security

Password
High security

- Go through the prompt again to add the fingerprint lock code.
- Afterward, press "**Done**."

Fingerprint added

Add another fingerprint?

Add   Done

||| ○   ‹

- Press the appropriate settings to turn it on or off.
- To disable the lock screen, press "**Screen lock type**." Go ahead and enter the additional lock code you added during the setup.
- Thereafter, touch "**None**."
- After that, press "**Remove data**."

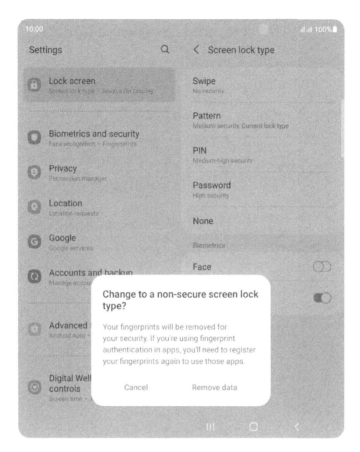

- Lastly, press "**Remove**."

Update Software

To ensure your smartphone has the newest operating system and features, try to update the firmware once there's an update.

- Head to the Settings app.

- Right there, press "**Software update**."

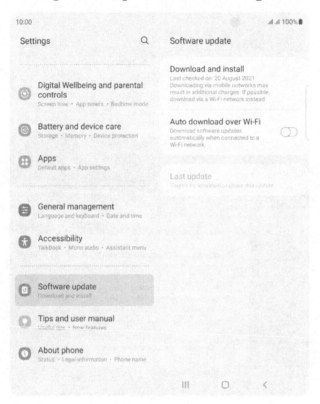

- Next up, press "**Download and install**."
- If Samsung releases a new firmware version, it'll display.
- Go through the guide to complete the update.

Enable RAM Plus

With RAM Plus, you can optimize your smartphone for an extra 4GB of memory.

- Launch the Settings app.
- Next up, press "**Battery and device care**."
- Thereafter, touch "**Memory**."
- After this, press "**RAM Plus**."
- Go ahead and select your desired option.
- Next up, press "**Restart now**."

Chapter Four

Add Email Accounts to Galaxy Flip

Adding an email account to your Galaxy Flip is easy. With it, you can send and receive emails, as well as back up and sync your data.

Add a Samsung Account
- Head to the Settings app.
- Thereafter, press "**Samsung account**."
- Follow up by inserting your Samsung account details to sign in.
- Press "**Create account**" to register for an account if you don't have one already.

Add a Google Account
- Head to the Settings app.
- Thereafter, press "**Accounts and backup**."
- After that, touch "**Manage accounts**."
- Right after, choose "**Add account**."
- Then, press "**Google**."
- Go ahead and insert your Google account details to register for an account.

Adding an Email Account

If you're using another email provider that is different from the above two, then do this.

- Head to the Settings app.
- Thereafter, press "**Accounts and backup**."
- Next up, touch "**Manage accounts**."
- After this, press "**Add account**."
- Follow up by pressing your email provider and inserting your account information.
- Go through the guide to complete it.

Delete an Account

If you no longer need any of the accounts, you can just delete them.

- Head to the Settings app.
- Thereafter, press "**Accounts and backup**."
- Next up, touch "**Manage accounts**."
- Then, tap the desired account.
- From this, press "**Remove account**."
- Go through the guide to complete it.

Chapter Five

Add Fingerprint Security

By adding a fingerprint to your smartphone, you can ensure nobody will be able to unlock it unless you have their fingerprint registered on your Galaxy Flip or you use yours to unlock it for them.

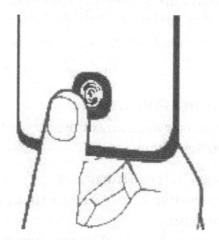

- Head to the Settings app.
- Next up, touch "**Biometrics and security**."
- After this, press "**Fingerprints**."
- Follow up by inserting your lock screen credential. If there's none, you may be required to create one.
- After this, choose "**Continue**."
- Go through the guide to add your fingerprint.
- After it's completed, press "**Done**."

- Click the toggle beside the "**Fingerprint unlock**" option to activate it.

Enable Additional Fingerprints

To add another fingerprint of yours or that of another person on your Galaxy Flip, you can do so from the same menu.

- Head to the Settings app.
- Next up, touch "**Biometrics and security**."
- After this, press "**Fingerprints**."
- Proceed by entering your screen lock credentials, then press "**Add fingerprint**."
- Thereafter, choose "**Done**."

Delete a Fingerprint

- Head to the Settings app.
- Next up, touch "**Biometrics and security**."
- Thereafter, press "**Fingerprints**."
- Insert your screen lock credentials, then press the fingerprint you intend to delete.

- Then, choose "**Remove**."
- Afterward, press "**Remove**" once more.

Add Face Recognition

By adding your face to your smartphone, your Galaxy Flip will only unlock once it detects your face, making sure that nobody encroaches on your files.

- Head to the Settings app.
- Next up, touch "**Biometrics and security**."
- Thereafter, press "**Face recognition**."
- Then, touch "**Continue**."
- Go through the guide and position your smartphone some inches away, then position your face within the frame. Do that until the progress bar gets to 100%.
- Then, touch "**OK**."

Delete Face Recognition

- Head to the Settings app.
- Next up, touch "**Biometrics and security**."
- Thereafter, press "**Face recognition**."

- Go ahead and enter the lock type to unlock the next menu.
- Next up, touch "**Remove face data**."
- Afterward, choose "**Remove**."

Chapter Six

Activate Touch Sensitivity

If your smartphone takes time to respond to touches after you put on a screen protector, try increasing the sensitivity.

- Launch the Settings app.
- Then, touch "**Display**."
- Thereafter, press "**Touch sensitivity**" and toggle it on.

Activate Touch and Hold Delay

To set the timeframe it takes for your smartphone to detect a touch-and-hold action, you can add the delay duration.

- Launch the Settings app.
- Then, select "**Accessibility**."
- Right there, touch "**Interaction and dexterity**."
- Thereafter, touch "**Touch and hold delay**."
- Follow up by touching your desired duration.

Adjust the Tap Duration

To set the timeframe it takes for your smartphone to detect a tap action, you can adjust the tap duration.

- Launch the Settings app.
- Then, select "**Accessibility**."
- Right there, touch "**Interaction and dexterity**."
- Thereafter, touch "**Tap duration**."
- Press the toggle to turn it on.
- Press the minus or plus button to adjust the duration.

Activate Ignore Repeated Touches

You can adjust how long it takes for two consecutive taps on the display to be counted as separate touches.

- Launch the Settings app.
- Then, select "**Accessibility**."
- Right there, touch "**Interaction and dexterity**."
- Thereafter, touch "**Ignore repeated touches**."

- Press the toggle to turn it on.
- Touch the minus or plus button to adjust the duration.

Activate Accidental Touch Protection

Turning on Accidental touch protection ensures that you protect your smartphone against unintended touches.

- Launch the Settings app.
- Then, select "**Display**."
- Thereafter, touch "**Accidental touch protection**."
- Touch the toggle to enable it.

Activate Finger Sensor Gesture

With the Finger Sensor Gesture, you can swiftly access the Notification panel on your smartphone.

- Head to the Settings app.
- Next up, touch "**Advanced Features**."

- Thereafter, touch "**Motion Gestures**."
- Touch the "**Finger Sensor Gestures**" option and toggle it on.

Activate Double-tap

If you wish to wake your phone whenever you double-tap on the display, then you should turn on this feature.

- Head to the Settings app.
- Right there, choose "**Advanced features**."
- Thereafter, choose "**Motions and gestures**."
- Touch the switch beside the "**Double tap**" tile.

Activate Lift to Wake

- Head to the Settings app.
- Thereafter, touch "**Motions and Gestures**."
- Right there, touch "**Lift to wake**."
- Press the switch beside the "**Lift to wake**" tile to toggle it on.

Change the Screen Layout

- Head to the Settings app.
- Next up, touch "**Display**."
- After this, touch "**Screen layout and zoom**."
- Follow up by pressing "**Multi view**" or "**Standard view**."
- Proceed by dragging the bar horizontally to adjust the display zoom.

Activate Extra Dim

With Extra Dim, you can decrease the brightness of your Galaxy Flip below what is normally achievable.

- Launch the Settings app.
- Right there, select "**Accessibility**."
- Thereafter, touch "**Visibility enhancements**."
- Afterward, touch "**Extra dim**."
- Touch the toggle to enable the **Extra dim** option.
- Proceed by dragging the slider horizontally to adjust the screen's intensity.

Lock your Home Screen

If you always unintentionally mess up your phone's home screen layout, you can lock it to prevent this from happening again.

- Head to the Settings app.
- Then, touch "**Home screen**."
- Touch the switch beside the "**Lock Home screen layout**" tile to toggle it on.

Chapter Seven

Set up the Samsung Wallet

With the Samsung Wallet, users can store their gift cards, debit cards, and so on. The app also features It incorporates Samsung Pay.

- Launch the Samsung Wallet app.
- Read the displayed information, then choose "**Continue.**"
- Follow up by inserting your Samsung account credentials, and then selecting "**Continue.**"
- Go ahead and add your fingerprints if you haven't done so. Touch the "**Register fingerprints**" button and go through the prompt.
- Position your finger on the fingerprint sensor to authenticate.
- From the prompt, press "**All the time**" or "**Don't use.**"
- Thereafter, press "**Done.**"
- Go through the guide to complete it.

Adding a Payment Method

After setting up the Wallet app, you can then add your debit card, boarding passes, etc.

- Head to the Samsung Wallet app.
- Touch the three dots at the right.
- Then, choose Payment cards.

- Touch the plus button at the upper right edge.
- Thereafter, choose your desired registration method.
- Go through the prompt to add your cards.

Set up Samsung Pass

Samsung Pass is a handy tool for storing your multiple account credentials and logging you into services (such as applications and websites) without having to enter them manually.

- Head to the Samsung Wallet app.
- Touch the three dots button on the right.
- Press the gear icon.
- Touch the toggle beside the "**Autofill with Samsung Keyboard**" option to enable it.
- Head to your application/website.
- Try signing into the app as you would usually do. You should now see the Samsung Pass memo asking if you prefer to save your login details. Touch "**Save**."
- When next you try to sign into that app, Samsung Pass will automatically fill in your sign-in credentials. Press your desired account, and use your fingerprint to authenticate your identity.

Personalize Accounts on Samsung Pass

- Launch the Samsung Wallet app.
- Right there, press the Menu tab.
- Move down to view the "**Samsung Pass**" section.
- Thereafter, touch "**Sign-in info**."
- Proceed by confirming your identity via fingerprint. From here, you can access all your saved logins with Samsung Pass.
- Touch "**Manual**" to manually add new credentials. Afterward, touch the plus icon.
- Follow up by inserting your account credentials.
- Then, touch "**Save**."

Adjust Notifications for Samsung Wallet

You can adjust the notification settings for the Samsung Wallet app to your liking.

- Launch the Samsung Wallet app.
- Touch the Menu tab.
- Touch the gear icon at the upper right edge.
- Thereafter, touch "**Notifications**."
- After that, press "**Notification categories**."
- Touch the toggle beside your desired notification types to enable or disable it.

Chapter Eight

Enable Bixby Voice

If you prefer to navigate and interact with your smartphone with just voice commands, then you should consider setting up Bixby Voice.

- Long-tap the Side key of your Galaxy Flip to access Bixby.
- If you need to change Bixby's language, touch "**English (United States)**" on the upper right edge. From there, touch your desired language.
- After this, press "**Start**."
- Thereafter, choose "**OK**."
- Once the setup is over, long-tap the Side key again to invoke and interact with Bixby. If desired, you can just open the Bixby app from the application list.

Delete Bixby Account

Removing your Bixby account will not uninstall the Bixby app; rather, all the information related to your Bixby account will be erased.

- Launch the Bixby app.
- Touch the three horizontal lines.
- Thereafter, press the gear icon.

- Afterward, choose "**Privacy**."
- Then, press "**Leave Bixby**."
- After this, choose "**Leave Bixby**" again.
- Next up, touch "**OK**."
- Follow up by inserting your Samsung account data.
- Afterward, touch "**OK**."
- Proceed to sign in to your Samsung account.
- After this, press "**Bixby Voice**" to erase it.

View Bixby Routines

Bixby routine enables you to automate certain tasks.

- Head to the Settings app.
- Then, touch "**Advanced features**."
- Next up, press "**Bixby Routines**."

Enable Common Routines

- Head to the Settings app.
- Then, touch "**Advanced features**."
- Afterward, touch "**Bixby Routines**."
- Next up, choose the "**Discover**" tab.

- Touch on a routine to customize it.
- Touch "**Edit**" to customize additional settings.
- After this, press "**Next**."
- Select your preferred routine name, then go ahead to pick a color and an icon.
- Then, press "**Done**."

Add Custom Routine

- Launch the Settings app.
- Then, touch "**Advanced features**."
- Afterward, touch "**Bixby Routines**."
- After that, press the "**Add routine**" tab.
- Select the avatar underneath "**If**."
- Follow up by touching an option from the trigger list, then go through the prompt if required.
- After that, select the avatar underneath "**Then**."
- Then, touch the action you need to perform.
- When the timer on the trigger runs out, the process will end. Additionally, it will reset all customized preferences to their original values. To disable it, select "**Reverse these actions**" and then flip the switch next to it.
- Thereafter, touch "**Next**."
- Afterward, choose "**Done**."

Add Parental Controls

With Parental Control, you can limit the duration you or your kid spends using your Galaxy Flip smartphone.

- Head to the Settings app.
- Afterward, press "**Digital Wellbeing and parental controls**."
- Right there, press "**Parental controls**."
- Then, touch "**Get started**."
- Proceed by choosing "**Teen**," "**Parent**," or "**Child**." Select depending on whose device it is. Touch "**Parent**."
- Thereafter, touch "**Get Family Link**."
- Go through the prompts to download the Google Family Link application for parents.
- Once the installation is finished, press "**Open**."
- Afterward, touch "**Get started**."
- Go ahead and choose your desired Google accounts, if you're using multiple accounts on the smartphone.
- Follow up by selecting who'll use the smartphone; "**Teen**," "**Parent**," or "**Child**." Touch "**Parent**."
- Ensure both devices are nearby, then press "**Next**."
- After this, choose "**I'm ready**."

- Next up, touch "**Yes**" or" **No**."
- Thereafter, choose "**Next**" to set up your child's smartphone.
- Proceed by using your child's device to install the Google Family Link for kids and youths.
- Go ahead and insert the Family Link setup code.
- Go through the guide to finish the setup.

Disable Supervising an Account

If your kid is 13 years old, you'll be able to stop supervising their account.

- From the supervisor's smartphone, head to the Google Family Link application.
- Thereafter, choose the kid's account that you intend to stop supervising.
- Underneath "**Settings**," choose "**Manage**."
- After this, choose "**Account info**."
- Thereafter, touch "**Stop supervision**."
- Go through the prompt.

Activate Game Launcher

To play games on your smartphone without being interrupted by notifications, setting up the game launcher will help.

- Head to the Settings app.
- After this, touch "**Advanced features**."
- Go ahead and press the switch beside the "**Game Launcher**" option to activate it.
- Launch the Game Launcher app.
- In there, press "**Allow**."
- To keep your game apps away from the application list, mark the "**Show games in Game Launcher only**" box. Press the three horizontal lines, then touch "**Settings**." After this, press "**Show games apps**." Thereafter, choose your desired option.
- Head back to the Game Launcher home menu, then touch any of the games to start playing it.

Copy and Paste across Samsung Galaxy Devices

If you own multiple Samsung devices, you can copy and paste from one of them to another wirelessly without a cable connection. Just ensure the devices are using the same Samsung account. Then, enable Bluetooth on the two devices. You should also ensure that they're paired with the same Wi-Fi connection.

- Head to the Settings app.
- Thereafter, touch "**Advanced features**."
- Press the switch beside "**Continue apps on other devices**" to have the feature enabled.
- Perform the above action on the other device. With this, you'll be able to copy and paste content across the two devices.

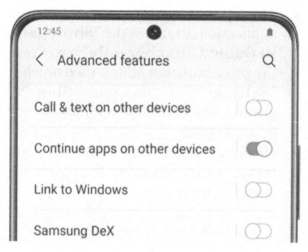

- Long-press a text on one of the devices, then press "**Copy**." Right on the second device, long-press on the input field, then touch "**Paste**."

Set up Dual Messenger

With Dual Messenger, you'll be able to have two different accounts for the same application. For instance, you can operate two WhatsApp, Twitter, or Facebook accounts from one phone.

- Head to the Settings app.
- Right there, press "**Advanced features**."
- After that, press "**Dual Messenger**."
- Touch the switch beside the available app.
- Thereafter, press "**Install**."
- After this, press "**Confirm**."
- Navigate to the newly downloaded version of the app, you'll see the Dual Messenger sign on it.
- Proceed by filling in your credentials to begin different accounts of the same app.

Import a PDF

Samsung Notes app makes the transfer of PDF files to the Galaxy Flip very easy.

- Launch the Samsung Notes app.
- Touch the PDF icon.
- Follow up by choosing a folder, then select your desired PDF file.
- Then, select "**Done**."
- Proceed by inserting text or drawings into the file.

Export a PDF

- Launch the Samsung Notes app.
- Navigate to the note you wish to export.
- Touch the three vertical dots.
- Then, select "**Save as file**."
- After that, select "**PDF file**."
- Proceed by browsing the folder you prefer to save the file.
- Thereafter, press the plus icon to create a new folder.
- Afterward, touch "**Save**."
- If you need to remove it, press the three vertical dots, then select "**Delete**." From there, press "**Move to Trash**."

Chapter Nine

Set up SmartThings App

With the SmartThings app, you'll be able to control and track your smart home devices like light bulbs, vacuum cleaners, TVs, thermostats, and more.

- Head to the SmartThings app.
- Right there, choose "**Continue**."
- Afterward, touch "**Continue**" again.
- Proceed by authorizing the required permissions.
- Once you've set up the application, you can begin importing devices to it.

Add Devices

To start controlling smart home devices, you'll have to add them first to the app.

- Head to the SmartThings app.
- Then, press the "**Devices**" tab.

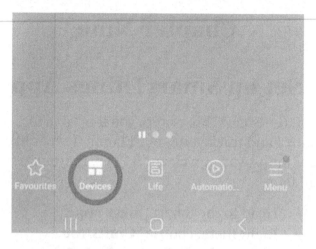

- Touch the home icon.
- Go ahead and select your desired location for the device.
- After this, choose the plus icon.
- Next up, touch "**Add device**."
- For Bluetooth-compatible devices, touch "**Scan nearby**."

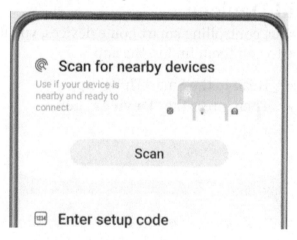

- Go ahead and pick the device once it appears. If it doesn't display, go ahead and add it manually. For Samsung appliances, touch "**By device type**" to pick the type of appliance. If not, select "**By brand**." If needed, use the search field to find a device.

- Go through the guide to pair the device with the SmartThings app.

Remove Devices

- Head to the SmartThings app.
- Touch the "**Devices**" tab.
- Next up, press the Home icon.
- Go ahead and select where the device is located.
- Select the device.
- Afterward, press the three vertical dots.
- Then, press "**Edit**."
- Next up, touch "**Delete device**."
- After this, choose "**Delete**."

Manage Devices

After adding an appliance to the SmartThings app, you can start tracking or controlling it from there.

- Launch the SmartThings app.
- Touch the "**Devices**" tab.
- After that, press the Home icon.
- Then, select the device's location.
- Touch the device.

- Afterward, press the dropdown menu.
- Next up, select "**All devices**."
- Follow up by making your desired adjustments.

Chapter Ten

Set up your Samsung Health Profile

For health and fitness fanatics, the Samsung Health app offers a simple way to monitor your exercises, heart rate, and digital well-being.

s

Sign in to Samsung Account

- Head to the Samsung Health application.
- Proceed to log in, If you're not already, then go through the prompt.
- Next up, touch "**Agree**."
- Afterward, choose "**Continue**."
- Thereafter, press "**Next**."
- Now, touch "**Continue**."
- Proceed by granting the needed permissions.
- Follow up by choosing the phone number that will be linked to your Samsung Health account.
- After that, choose "**Next**."
- Then, choose "**Agree**."
- Go through the guide to finalize.

Customize your Data

On the "**Edit**" menu of the Samsung Health application, 'you'll be able to adjust certain personal data.

- Launch the Samsung Health app.
- Afterward, press the "**My Page**" tab.
- Thereafter, touch the "**Edit**" tile next to your name.
- Follow up by changing data such as your weight, avatar, height, etc.
- Afterward, choose "**Save**."
- To log out, press the three vertical dots. Then, choose "**Settings**." Next up, choose the "**Samsung account**." Afterward, choose "**Sign out**." Go through the guide to sign out.

Manage your Digital Wellbeing

With Digital Wellbeing, you'll be able to limit your usage of individual applications to a specific period every day.

Add Goals

If there's a duration you wish to only spend on your smartphone, you can add your screen time goal to the Digital Wellbeing menu.

- Head to the Settings app.
- Thereafter, touch "**Digital Wellbeing and parental controls**."
- Right there, touch "**Digital Wellbeing**."
- Next up, touch "**Screen time**" underneath "**Your goals**."
- Afterward, choose "**Set goal**."
- Go ahead and choose your screen time goal.
- After which, press "**Done**."

Add App Timer

You can add the duration you wish to spend on certain applications daily.

- Head to the Settings app.
- Next up, press "**Digital Wellbeing and parental controls**."
- Right there, press "**Digital Wellbeing**."
- Afterward, choose "**App timers**" underneath "**Your goals**."
- Touch the hourglass icon next to your look-for app.
- Follow up by selecting your desired duration.
- Afterward, touch "**Done**."

Turn on Bedtime Mode

The Bedtime mode informs you when it's time to go to bed.

- Head to the Settings app.
- After this, press "**Digital Wellbeing and parental controls**."
- Right there, choose "**Digital Wellbeing**."
- Next up, press "**Bedtime mode**."
- If prompted, choose "**Start**."
- Press the switch next to the "**Turn on as scheduled**" option to enable it.
- Follow up by selecting the days to make use of Bedtime mode.
- Next up, touch "**Set schedule**."
- Choose the time.
- After that, choose "**Done**."
- Thereafter, choose "**OK**."

Activate Focus Mode

The Focus mode helps you stay on track when working on an important task. It enables you to fully focus and keep away from all distractions, such as incoming notifications.

- Head to the Settings app.
- After this, press "**Digital Wellbeing and parental controls**."

- Right there, choose "**Digital Wellbeing**."
- Underneath "Focus mode," touch any of the listed options, then edit it to your liking.

Chapter Eleven

Enable Flex Mode

Once Flex mode is turned on and your Galaxy Flip is folded and standing vertically, whatever applications you're using will now show at the top of the display. You should now see a panel with extra buttons at the bottom of the device.

- Launch the Settings app.
- In there, touch "**Advanced features**."
- After this, choose "**Labs**."
- Thereafter, choose "**Flex mode panel**."
- Follow up by pressing the switch next to an application to activate its Flex mode panel.
- Afterward, launch the app.
- Proceed by folding your smartphone to see the application in Flex mode.
- The Flex mode panel will now show at the bottom section of the display. You can use the panel to change sound, capture screenshots, adjust notifications, etc.

Edit the Navigation Bar

At the bottom of the Galaxy Flip, you'll see the navigation bar, consisting of three onscreen buttons: the middle button is the Home button, the right represents the Back button, and at the right, you have the Recent Apps button.

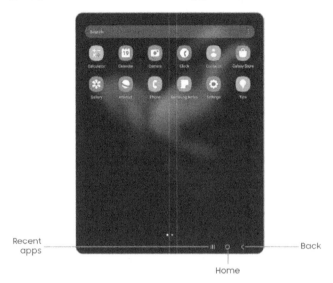

Recent apps — Home — Back

Change the Navigation Bar Type

If you would rather use the swipe gesture instead of the navigation bar to navigate your smartphone, you can adjust the settings.

- Launch the Settings app.
- In there, choose "**Display**."
- After that, choose "**Navigation bar**."
- Thereafter, touch "**Swipe gestures**" or "**Navigation buttons**."

- To fully hide the Swipe gestures outlines, toggle off "**Gesture hints**."

Change the Swipe Gestures

You can make the buttons that display on the navigation bar go away.

- Head to the Settings app.
- Then, press "**Display**."
- Thereafter, choose "**Navigation bar**."
- Next up, press "**Swipe gestures**."
- Hit on the switch next to "**Gesture hints**" to enable it and get help on where to swipe.
- Press the toggle beside the "**Show button**" option.
- Press "**More options**" to personalize the direction you've to swipe.

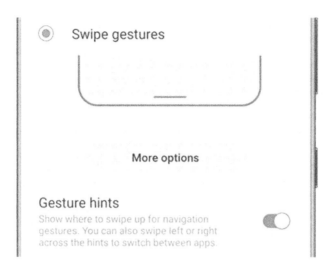

Swipe gestures

More options

Gesture hints

Show where to swipe up for navigation
gestures. You can also swipe left or right
across the hints to switch between apps.

Change the Navigation Bar Location

If you need to adjust the position of the buttons on the Navigation bar, you can do it with ease.

- Launch the Settings app.
- Thereafter, touch "**Display**."
- After this, touch the "**Navigation bar**."
- Then, choose "**Button position**."

- Proceed by choosing your desired button settings.

Turn on the Taskbar

You can toggle on the taskbar menu and have your recent applications also displayed at the bottom of your smartphone.

Shortcuts ——— Recent apps

Apps list ———

- Head to the Settings app.
- Next up, touch "**Display**."
- After this, press "**Taskbar**."

- Hit on ⬤ to turn on the taskbar.

- Press ⬤ to also enable **Show recent apps**.

Activate Screen Zoom

On the Screen Zoom menu, you can drag the slider to make the content on your smartphone appear larger than it is.

- Launch the Settings app.

- Hit on **"Display."**
- Next up, select **"Screen Zoom."**
- Follow up by dragging the slider at the bottom horizontally.

Activate Full-Screen Apps

You can make certain applications take up the whole screen while using them.

- Launch the Settings app.
- Right there, press **"Display."**
- Next up, touch **"Full-screen apps."**
- Thereafter, press **"Camera cutout"** or **"Aspect ratio."**
- Follow up by selecting your desired app.

Enable Easy Mode

If you find the display of your smartphone a little bit advanced, you can toggle on Easy Mode to make it easier and more intuitive.

- Launch the Settings app.
- Then, choose **"Display."**
- Thereafter, press **"Easy mode."**
- Touch the toggle to enable it.

Activate LED Edge Notification Light

Edge light brightens up the edges of your smartphone whenever you receive an alert.

- Head to the Settings app.
- Then, select "**Notifications**."
- Thereafter, touch "**Brief pop-up settings**."
- Next up, select an Edge lighting style.
- Then, choose your desired edge lighting effect.

Enable Flash Notification

With flash notification turned on, you'll get a flash notification on your smartphone once you receive an alert.

- Navigate to the Settings app.
- Right there, touch "**Notifications**."
- Thereafter, touch "**Flash notification**" below the "**Looking for something else?**" heading.
- To ensure that your smartphone flashes the camera when you get an alert, press

the toggle beside the "**Camera flash notification**" option.

- To make your phone's screen flash when an alert comes in, toggle on "**Screen flash notification.**"

Chapter Twelve

Set up Secure Folder

To keep sensitive information hidden from people to whom you give your smartphone, you can store it in the Secure Folder. To prevent unauthorized access, add a security option to it.

Creating a Secure Folder

- Head to the Settings app.
- Right there, press "**Biometrics and security**."
- Next up, touch "**Secure Folder**."
- Follow up by signing into your Samsung Account. Otherwise, create one.
- Then, choose "**Sign in**."
- Follow up by inserting your Samsung Account details.
- Then, press "**Sign in**"
- Go ahead and choose your desired lock type, then press "**Next**."
- After selecting the lock type, press "**Continue**."
- Go through the lock method again, then press "**Confirm**." The Secure Folder shortcut will display on your application screen.

Adding Files to Secure Folder

After creating the Secure Folder, you can transfer files to it.

- Head to the Secure Folder app.
- Press the three dots.
- Then, press "**Add files**."
- Follow up by choosing the file type you intend to add.
- Then, select the files.
- After that, press "**Done**."
- Go ahead and choose to move or copy the files.

Add Apps to Secure Folder

- Head to the Secure Folder app.
- Press the plus icon or choose "**Add Apps**."
- Follow up by selecting the applications you intend to add.
- Next up, choose "**Add**."

View your Items in the Secure Folder

You can view the Gallery contents you moved to the secure folder.

- Head to the Secure Folder app.
- Next up, press "**Gallery**" to see your images.

- Select "**My Files**" to access your files.

Hide the Secure Folder

To ensure your secure folder doesn't show on your home or application screen, you can hide it.

- Head to the Settings app.
- Right there, press "**Biometrics and security**."
- Next up, press "**Secure Folder**."
- Follow up by pressing the toggle beside the "**Show icon on Apps screen**" option.
- After that, press "**Hide**."

Access the Hidden Secure Folder

- Drag down from the top of your Galaxy Flip with two fingers. This will launch the Quick menu.
- Follow up by swiping right, then press the plus button.
- Swipe right once more.
- Drag and drop the Secure Folder into the Quick menu.
- Hit on the Secure Folder icon to hide or reveal it.

Delete Secure Folder

- Head to the Settings app.
- Right there, press **"Biometrics and security."**
- Next up, choose **"Secure Folder."**
- Select the three dots or choose **"More settings."**
- After this, press **"Uninstall."**
- Next up, choose **"Uninstall"** once more.

Chapter Thirteen

Samsung Internet App

With Samsung's Internet app, you can surf the internet in private mode and even clear cache and block ads, among other things.

Enable Private Browsing

By switching to private browsing, you ensure that none of your data is saved whenever you're surfing the internet.

- Launch the Samsung Internet app.
- Press the that has a number icon.
- After that, touch "**Turn on Secret mode**."
- Thereafter, choose "**Start**."

Remove Cache, History, and Cookies

By deleting your cache and cookies, you're ensuring that no website will track your online browsing activities.

- Head to the Samsung Internet app.
- Touch the three horizontal lines.
- Then, touch "**Settings**."
- Next up, touch "**Personal browsing data**."

- Thereafter, touch "**Delete browsing data**."
- Choose Cookies, History to clear.
- Right there, select "**Delete data**."
- Afterward, touch "**Delete**."

Install Ad Blockers

Ad blockers help prevent you from seeing advertising online if you find it unpleasant.

- Head to the Samsung Internet app.
- Touch the three horizontal lines.
- After this, touch "**Ad blockers**."
- Press the download icon beside your desired ad blocker.
- Thereafter, press "**Install**."
- Go back to the ad blockers settings menu, then press the toggle beside your desired ad blocker to turn it on.
- Whenever you're surfing the internet, press the three horizontal lines, and you should see the ad blockers icon with the number of blocked ads.

Conclusion

The Galaxy Flip 5 doesn't differ too much from the previous iteration but is somewhat restyled and uses the Android 13 OS. It's still a decent device that offers a lot to improve your productivity.

This book should get you up and running so you can start using your Galaxy Flip comfortably.

About the Author

Shawn Blaine is a gadget reviewer, programmer, and computer geek. He has worked for some big tech companies in the past. He's currently focused on coding and blockchain development but still finds time to write and teach people how to use their smart devices to the fullest.

Index

W

Made in the USA
Las Vegas, NV
10 February 2024

85602233R00066